WISE
CHOICES

G000059610

What the Bible Says about

GOING OUT,
MARRIAGE AND SEX

DR CHRIS RICHARDS DR LIZ JONES

*'Get wisdom, get understanding; do not forget my words
or swerve from them.
Do not forsake wisdom, and she will protect you; love her,
and she will watch over you.
Wisdom is supreme; therefore get wisdom.
Though it cost you all you have, get understanding.'*

Proverbs 4:5-7

DayOne

Foreword

I once saw a cartoon that depicted a group of people walking around on their hands, as if that was the norm. One guy was walking on his feet. Those on their hands were shouting at him, 'Odd ball!'

It has never been easy to swim against the tide, but the need to do so is something that both fish and Christians have in common. I am not sure that purity has ever been popular, but it is God's passionate desire for us, his people. Purity is not the goal of the media, or sadly, of the masses, and certainly not of Satan. Yet God calls us to follow him, in every area of our lives, and one of the most challenging of these is the realm of sexuality. We were beautifully, delicately, intricately created as sexual beings, but we are so quickly marred when we disregard the instructions God has given us, which are for our well-being.

The Lord, who gave us sexual desire, is willing to also give the desire and strength to live as he knows is best for us. God's standards and commands in the Bible are not there to frustrate us, but to protect us and liberate us from the pressures of society. To go God's way, though, is to swim against the flow that most follow. A generation ago, children in Sunday School sang used to sing:

> Dare to be a Daniel
> Dare to stand alone
> Dare to have a purpose true
> And dare to make it known.

It's the last line that is the hardest. To believe what others don't believe is fairly easy, but to argue the point is costly. Dr Chris Richards and Dr Liz Jones have dared to tell it is as it is, by honestly and frankly explaining what the Bible teaches on sex and relationships. The world may not be going to treat them as heroes, but if it helps us all to live as God wants us to, then we have much for which to thank them.

Roger Carswell

3

This book gives straight, honest answers to the many questions young people have about love, sex and relationships. It is clearly written, with plenty of real life examples. The authors show that when we trust God with every aspect of our lives, then we find real and lasting happiness.

Sharon James
Author and speaker

Sex can be great when used properly, but so damaging when we ignore the Maker's instructions. Christian teenagers and young people desperately need to know why it makes sense to wait until marriage before having sex, why the messages from the media and society are so dangerous, what are the consequences of getting it wrong and how they can learn, not to deny their sexuality, but to channel it in a way that pleases God and avoids pain and regret. This booklet is a clear and excellent summary of how the Bible's teaching can be applied faithfully and sensibly within a society that has hardly any moral direction. I thoroughly recommend it.

Dr Mark Pickering
Christian Medical Fellowship

Why is it such a big issue?

Nothing that we do can make us right before God; only the work of Jesus on the cross can do this. Christians are not saved by what they do, but they are saved for a life of holiness through obedience. Our desire for holiness is not an add-on, but the very heart of our daily walk with our Heavenly Father. We are warned that *'without holiness no-one will see the Lord'* (Hebrews 12:14). The Bible repeatedly reminds us that our thoughts and actions in relationships really matter to the God who commanded us to *'love your neighbour as yourself'* (Matthew 22:39).

As young people living in the twenty-first century, your pursuit of holiness is under intense attack. There is a battle on in our hearts between the attraction of the ways of the world and obedience to God (Galatians 5:17). Unless we are properly prepared for the battle, it is so easy to be drawn away by the world's loud voice. This takes the form of a steady drip feed of messages to which we are exposed every day. Here are just a few of them:

▶ 'Sex is everything in life and about self-fulfilment.'
▶ 'Marriage is old-fashioned.'
▶ 'Sex is a game.'
▶ 'There are no rights and wrongs in relationships, just what we prefer.'
▶ 'Sex can be experienced without consequences.'
▶ 'To have sex is to love and a means of securing love.'

> **As young people living in the twenty-first century, your pursuit of holiness is under intense attack. There is a battle on in our hearts between the attraction of the ways of the world and obedience to God.**
>
> *SEE GALATIANS 5:17*

All the messages above are lies or half-truths but they are also powerful and tempting.

We, as Christians, need to be on our guard. We need to know exactly what we believe and why, so that we can respond wisely and swiftly to difficult situations as they arise. However, we are not alone in this struggle! God has given us his Word, the Bible, and he equips us through the Holy Spirit who helps us understand his Word, and who motivates us and strengthens us.

Even when we are obedient, God does not necessarily give us all our desires straight away. He often gets us to wait, and, as we wait, he strengthens us and teaches us patience until he fulfils our desires in his time. It may seem hard to obey and to wait. That is part of faith—trusting that his provision and timing are best.

> **Though we can receive complete forgiveness for our disobedience, we may have to live with the earthly consequences for the rest of our lives. Nowhere is this clearer than in God's gift of sex.**

The Bible also warns us that the stakes of obedience are high and the consequences of disobedience can be severe. Though we can receive complete forgiveness for our disobedience, we may have to live with the earthly consequences for the rest of our lives. Nowhere is this clearer than in God's gift of sex.

We hope that this booklet will help you to know more about God's ways and desires for you in this area of your life. Our prayer is that it will help you *'make level paths for your feet and take only ways that are firm'* (Proverbs 4:26).

We begin by mentioning something that we have all experienced, no matter what stage in life we are at…

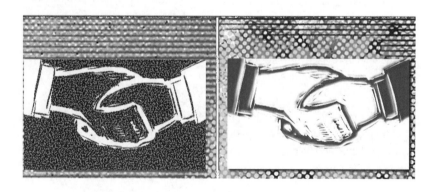

First things first

FRIENDSHIP

Without friendship, this is a very lonely world. Throughout his busy and demanding ministry, Jesus enjoyed the companionship and support of a small group of close friends, including Lazarus and his disciples, Peter, James and John. God intends us to know the blessings of friendship in our lives as well.

However, the Bible reminds us that those closest to us influence us most (Proverbs 13:20), so we should choose our friends carefully. Godly friends are the best of friends. We should nurture friendships with those who will stick by us in hardship (Proverbs 18:24), whom we can mutually encourage and support to work effectively for the Lord (Ecclesiastes 4:9-12), and who will challenge us when we make spiritually foolish decisions (Proverbs 27:6a). You can learn more about the qualities of a deep friendship by reading the moving account of David and Jonathan in 1 Samuel 20.

MARRIAGE—A SPECIAL FRIENDSHIP

Establishing deep friendships will be a great blessing in itself. They will also help you to know what to look for in a potential marriage partner since these same qualities are experienced at a deeper level in the unique relationship of marriage. God created marriage for companionship—he created Adam and observed, *'It is not good for the man to be alone'* (Genesis 2:18). So he also created Eve and then brought them together in this special way, which is to be a model for all future marriages. *'For this reason a man will leave his father and mother and be united to his wife, and they will become one flesh'* (Genesis 2:24).

Because marriage was created for friendship, it is important that the person you choose to marry should be your best friend. Furthermore, as Christians, we need to believe that God is sovereign in this area as he is in all areas of our lives; if he wishes us to marry, he has the perfect marriage partner lined up for us—a best friend of his choosing!

But marriage is friendship with a difference. God intends marriage to be life-long (Matthew 19:4-6) 'until death do us part' and with one person of the opposite sex (1 Corinthians 7:2) so that we are 'forsaking all others'. The depth and permanence of marriage demands that, as is said in the marriage vows, this way of life should not be undertaken 'carelessly, lightly or selfishly but reverently, responsibly and after serious thought'. The words of such commitment are to be said in public so that all the people know that they should respect and support this special relationship (Hebrews 13:4).

Sadly, we live in times when there are fewer good role models for marriage. Many of us come from families where marriages have failed and many church communities have experienced the tragic break-up of marriages within their midst. So, if or when you are thinking about marriage, make the most of learning from the secure and happy marriages that you see around you and take seriously the possibility of going together to a marriage preparation class.

Notice the order in the verse, *'For this reason a man will leave his father and mother and be united to his wife, and they will become one flesh'*. The order of events is no accident! The couple need to 'leave' their parental family unit as they marry—with parents actively letting go of their son or daughter—and the couple form a new family unit in a new place. And the couple need to 'be united' in marriage *before* they experience the act of sexual intercourse as *'the two become one flesh'*. With this gift of sex, God has given the married couple a unique source of strengthening and joy. With the gift of marriage, God has given us the one and only right context for sexual activity.

You may be thinking that marriage sounds a good if somewhat daunting prospect for some time in the future. But you may also be wondering just how you get to the point of deciding to marry someone, and what your attitude should be to sex until you decide to make those marriage vows. So let us then look in some detail at the issue of 'going out'.

GOING OUT

(Just to get any language misunderstandings out of the way at the start, by 'going out' we don't mean simply a one-off date, but a regular commitment to meet up with and get to know someone of the opposite sex. It actually means more than this, but read on!)

> **By 'going out' we don't mean simply a one-off date, but a regular commitment to meet up with and get to know someone of the opposite sex.**

You may feel a lot of pressure on you to go out with someone. The more that your friends pair off, the harder it is to be the one who doesn't. And if you don't go out, you may receive all kinds of hints that you are missing out or abnormal. As Christians, we should always be asking ourselves not only whether what we are doing is right but also whether it is wise. With so much pressure from modern society around, here are some observations to help you think about whether and with whom you should go out.

What does the Bible say about 'going out'?

'Going out', as we know it in our society, is not really spoken about in the Bible. God doesn't seem to give us a specific command about this state. This may be because of cultural differences between then and now. Amongst the people of Israel many marriages were arranged and prior to marriage there would have been a period of betrothal. Mary and Joseph were betrothed to be married. This is probably similar to being engaged—a preparation time that still allowed an opportunity to back out (which Joseph tried to do, until the angel told him not to). In the Bible this backing out is referred to as 'divorce' but it is not the same as divorce from marriage. There was no sexual intercourse at that point, as they weren't yet married. (Mary was pregnant, and Joseph knew it wasn't by him!)

The Bible may not speak of 'going out' as such but it does give a few examples of friendship between men and women that grew and led to marriage, for example that of Ruth and Boaz in the Book of Ruth. Notice how they 'check each other out'—not only regarding physical attraction (Ruth is aware of this as she follows

Naomi's advice to *'wash and perfume [herself], and put on [her] best clothes'*) (Ruth 3:3), but also their characters (e.g. Ruth 2:20 and 3:11). As their friendship grows, so does the seriousness of their future commitment.

What is 'going out'?

If the Bible doesn't refer to going out and gives only a few examples of a growing friendship leading to marriage, what conclusions can we draw? More specifically, we want to address the issue of how 'going out' relates to marriage.

By taking a moment to analyse what 'going out' is, we hope you will agree that it is more than simple friendship with someone of the opposite sex. Going out has certain qualities which include:

▶ Exclusivity (you don't go out with two people at the same time);
▶ Public knowledge (some others will know about it);
▶ Physical/sexual attraction ;
▶ Some degree of intimacy (see below for some ways to be intimate without being arousing).

These qualities of 'going out' are shared with marriage and distinguish it from simple friendship. Therefore, we would argue that 'going out' should wisely be considered as a time of getting to know each other, in order to test out if marriage is a future possibility. To put it the other way round, if you could never imagine marrying him or her then you shouldn't be going out with that person. Obviously the certainty with which you can assess this will vary with how well you know him or her and how carefully you have thought through exactly what marriage is. That is why people go out with each other for a while rather than rushing into marriage.

> **'Going out' should wisely be considered as a time of getting to know each other, in order to test out if marriage is a future possibility.**

Perhaps you are surprised at this perspective! Did you plan to go out with several people in succession without any serious assessment of whether marriage is a possibility? Surely, you think, this can do no harm. Here are a few further points:

▶ Remember the amount of time and energy required for going out. Could the time and energy that is used on a series of (perhaps) short-term relationships be better spent with a whole range of needy or supportive friends or other work for God's Kingdom?

▶ *You* may think of a relationship as short term, but does your boy/girlfriend think the same? Misunderstanding about where the relationship is going can cause much hurt and waste of emotional energy. This is especially true if or when you decide to break up.

▶ Going out often makes people vulnerable to a new area of sexual temptation; this may not often be a definite reason against going out, but a reason to take it seriously and carefully.

▶ Most godly older Christians don't look back and say, 'I wish that I had been out with *more* people' but 'I wish I hadn't been out with *as many* people'!

The searching and the choosing[1]

It is tempting to spend a lot of time looking out for 'life's partner'. It can become *the* big priority in life. It may be reassuring to know that many Christians have had a sense of peaceful and exciting provision soon after meeting their future spouse. They can often look back to consider how the active searching had been hard work and fruitless, whilst finding had been blissfully effortless! This shouldn't be so surprising. We need to remember that there is a loving and sovereign God, who has an intimate knowledge of us, working 'behind the scenes' of our life. It is so easy for our searching to distract us from putting our energies into things of eternal importance. Jesus tells us to concentrate on God's kingdom and his righteousness, and all our needs will be met (Matthew 6:33).

Here is a quote from one famous missionary who found peace by placing this matter in God's hands:

'God always gives his very best to those who leave the choice with him.'
Hudson Taylor (1832-1905), missionary to China

In considering a relationship, appreciation of physical appearance is important. Men, especially, are initially attracted by appearance as well as by character. However, in our society which strongly emphasises the beautiful body, we need to be particularly careful of superficial assessments that only go skin deep. The guys tend to think of the girl for her suntan (which fades) and figure (which ages) without considering her *'inner self, the unfading beauty of a gentle and quiet spirit'* (1 Peter 3:4). The girls can be

> **God always gives his very best to those who leave the choice with him.**
>
> *HUDSON TAYLOR (1832-1905), MISSIONARY TO CHINA*

distracted by the thrill of attracting a man with their looks but then are disappointed when he only has a shallow interest in their character and well-being. Falling in love is a wonderful, God-given mystery and can help a couple to care for each other unselfishly. Feeling deeply for someone is important, but the love which survives the demands of marriage has a much stronger commitment than that drawn out by the first flush of feeling or appreciation for outer beauty.

As we have mentioned above, when thinking of going out, it is important to ask yourself whether you could imagine (or desire!) marrying that person at some stage in the future. Even early on you should have reservations about going out with someone if you could not answer the following questions positively:

▶ Can you entirely trust that person?
▶ Do they treat you with loyalty and respect? Is it easy to treat them with loyalty and respect?
▶ Do you sense they want what is best for you? Is it a joy to seek what is best for them?
▶ Have you got the potential to encourage each other to grow spiritually?

It is good to spend time together in the company of your biological and church families. Both of these may provide wise observations (though not the final say which is yours) about the suitability and quality of your relationship. Parents may have an important role here since they know more about you and your background than anyone else. Marriage is a family business! Going out is a time to consider how well you and your girl/boyfriend would get along with the greater family which you will join if you marry (without in any way compromising your future need and ability to form a new family unit when you do).

Marriage is a family business! Going out is a time to consider how well you and your girl/boyfriend would get along with the greater family which you will join if you marry.

Going out is also a time to think ahead to the tough realities of family life at close quarters for the rest of your days. Would

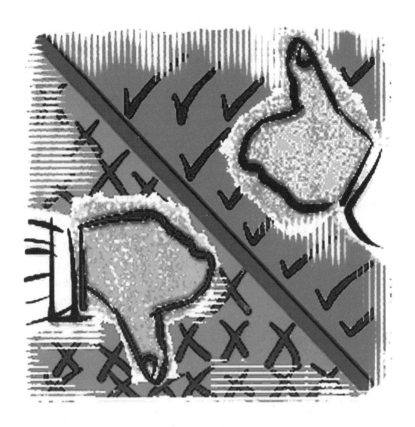

you want that person to be the parent of your child? Are you temperamentally and spiritually compatible? Do you share perspectives on issues such as money, work and health? As your relationship grows, you will need to think carefully about each of these areas.

Going out means selflessness!

'Be imitators of God, therefore, as dearly loved children, and live a life of love, just as Christ loved us and gave himself up for us as a fragrant offering and sacrifice to God' (Ephesians 5:1-2).

As with any other type of relationship, going out requires commitment to the other one in a loving and self-sacrificial way—just as Jesus loved us. So a girl/boyfriend is neither, for example, to be treated as an object to show off, nor manipulated for our own selfish ends. In contrast he or she is to be appreciated, encouraged, supported and built up in his or her spiritual life. That is quite a responsibility and another reason not to take going out lightly.

'There is far too much casualness, self-indulgence and unthinking selfishness masquerading as romantic love in relationships.'[2]

Right ways to attract and appreciate

So much in our culture tells us that the only way to show appreciation and win attraction is through sexual provocation or arousal. As we will explain later, this is unhelpful to a relationship and damaging to your spiritual life because it dishonours God. In contrast, whether going out or not, girls need to cultivate an attitude of modesty, which is referred to in 1 Timothy 2:9-10. This modesty is primarily directed towards men, and expressed through dress, actions and words. There is nothing wrong with displaying femininity attractively. The challenge is to do this in a way that is not sexually provocative.

For their part, guys need to radiate inner strength by striving for sexual purity. Testimonies indicate that it is more often guys who push the physical boundaries and many girls look back wishing that they had not gone as far as they had. They feel that it was expected of them and done to win them much desired affection, but in the wrong way. In these circumstances the girl should not feel shy about explaining this sense of pressure to her boyfriend. He needs to listen and respond lovingly by exercising self-control. Communication and thoughtfulness are vital at all stages of a relationship.

Without compromising these attitudes, it is good to be able to show appreciation and fondness to your girl/boyfriend. Here are six suggestions:

- Devoting time to thoughtful listening;
- Doing practical things to help;
- Expressing words of encouragement and appreciation;
- Giving presents;

▶ Giving careful physical affirmation—not aimed to arouse but encourage;

▶ Being devoted to praying for each other (not necessarily together).

You don't need to do all of these in the first week of the relationship! The challenge is to keep these expressions of appreciation and care in line with the depth and maturity of the relationship. Otherwise they can begin to lose their meaning. Which brings us to the next challenge of…

Using the emotional brakes

In addition to the physical self-control that we will mention again later, there is need for emotional self-control. It is possible to let the powerful emotions of being in love completely dominate your whole thinking and being. You need to control them rather than let them control you. These strong feelings can easily lead to a selfish preoccupation with each other that excludes other people. Such an attitude has damaged the community of many a youth group or college residence. You may also find yourself without the support of friends if your relationship breaks up.

If you are not careful, these powerful emotions can also lead you to make rash or unwise decisions. Peter warns us to *'be self-controlled and alert. Your enemy the devil prowls around like a roaring lion looking for someone to devour'* (1 Peter 5:8).

If you go gently, you will be able to make sure that your (and the other person's) actions and responses come from a sincere and steady heart and discover if there is a sense of increasing devotion to and fondness for each other. You will be able to avoid forcing a relationship in an unhelpful way through early intensity and a false closeness that is out of step with its maturity. How the relationship grows with time in an unpressurized environment is a good test of its quality.

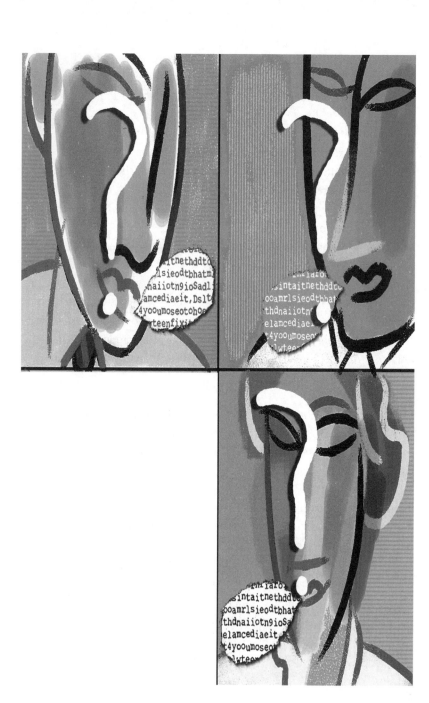

Three big questions

In this section we address the three questions that we are most often asked by young Christians on the subject of 'going out'.

ONE—Is it OK to go out with a non-Christian?

'Don't team up with those who are unbelievers. How can goodness be a partner with wickedness? How can light live with darkness? What harmony can there be between Christ and the devil? How can a believer be a partner with an unbeliever?' (2 Corinthians 6:14-15, New Living Translation)

> **If you decide to go out with a non-Christian, you will be ignoring God's Word and threatening your spiritual growth and peace.**

This passage applies to all close partnerships between the Christian and non-Christian and that certainly includes marriage and going out (which we have suggested should have the possibility of marriage in mind anyway). It is as stark as the passage describes—we are as different as light and darkness, good and evil. How can we ever be helpfully influenced by darkness or wickedness at close quarters? How can we ever be truly walking along the same path, sharing the same values, goals and understanding? If you decide to go out with a non-Christian, you will be ignoring God's Word and threatening your spiritual growth and peace. Here is Karen's testimony. She can look back over her years of marriage with mixed feelings. The regret of her early disobedience, with its years of spiritual pain and uncertainty, combine with thanks to God for bringing her and her husband to the blessings of their present situation:

Karen's story

As a Christian I had told God that I would follow him for ever, but instead of handing over full control of my life and plans to God, I insisted that I had to have a husband and a family. I desperately wanted to be loved and to love someone. I met a lovely man and even though I knew that, as a non-believer, he did not belong to God's kingdom of light, I married him, thinking that I could soon win him over to Jesus. At the time I did not think we were so very different, as I was well aware that my heart, though in God's kingdom of light, had many dark parts to it. I felt that my new husband's heart, though still in darkness, had some light in it as he had some good qualities!

In the early years of our marriage I was generally happy, though at times I felt frustrated and lonely because he could not share with me my deepest desire...for God. We had children and still he had not become a Christian. I feared he may die and not go to heaven. I worried that his lack of faith would damage our children's young faith in Jesus.

By God's grace, my husband became a Christian several years after we married. Since his conversion, I have felt relief from the single-handed responsibility of bringing up our children in God's love. It has also been very painful for us both to see that our relationship had lacked an honesty and depth that we can now have. I have grasped the massive difference in the hearts of believers and non-believers. When you have God's Spirit living in you, you are living in his light absolutely. Your heart is opposite to what it was.'

Like Karen, you may think that by going out you will eventually 'win them for Christ'. Karen turned out to be correct in predicting this but she had no way to be sure. God makes no promise that your non-Christian girl/boyfriend, husband or wife will come to faith. Sadly, her account is the exception. Usually the result is the other way round—the Christian leads a life that is spiritually isolated, frustrated by divided loyalties and a clash of life plans.

TWO—Does the Bible really say sex should be kept for marriage?
The Bible is consistent from beginning to end in its emphasis that sexual activity of any sort outside marriage is wrong.

As we have mentioned, God first placed sex within marriage and this is where he means it to remain! In the Old Testament virginity was expected of a bride, and

any sexual activity before marriage was described as that of a prostitute whether it was activity for money or not (Deuteronomy 22:20-21).

God first placed sex within marriage and this is where he means it to remain!

Having sex with a person who is married to somebody else is called adultery and is forbidden by God in the Old and New Testaments (Exodus 20:14 and Hebrews 13:4). If you are ever tempted to commit adultery, consider the severe and repeated warnings in Proverbs 5 to 7 about its social, financial and spiritual consequences. 'But a man who commits adultery lacks judgement; whoever does so destroys himself' (Proverbs 6:32).

There are many references to sex in the New Testament. In Matthew 19, Jesus outlines two (and only two) states for a life that pleases God—either married and sexually active, or single and sexually inactive. In this account Jesus is being cross-examined about the possibility of divorce. The disciples are shocked at the toughness of his reply, which maintains the permanence of marriage and the sin of adultery. They respond by exclaiming, *'If this is the situation between a husband and wife, it is better not to marry'* (verse 10), thinking perhaps that a looser non-marital sexual arrangement is the alternative to the demanding exclusivity of marriage. But they are in for another shock because the only alternative that Jesus gives to the state of marriage is that of a 'eunuch' i.e. someone who is compulsorily sexually inactive—either because he has no choice or because he has chosen to *'because of the kingdom of heaven'* (verse 12). Jesus gives no hint here of permitting pre-marital or extra-marital sex.

> **'But a man who commits adultery lacks judgement; whoever does so destroys himself.'**
> *(PROVERBS 6:32)*

Further direction to keep sex for marriage comes from the forbidding of 'sexual immorality' (e.g. 1 Corinthians 6:18, Ephesians 5:3). The word translated as 'immorality' in many modern versions means any sexual activity outside marriage including pre-marital sexual intimacy, adultery and homosexual acts.[3]

Common reasons given nowadays for not keeping sex for marriage
'We're planning to get married anyway'
Being obedient to God means doing the right things in the *right* order. We have already noted the order in the Genesis account of marriage. Sexual union comes after, not before, union in marriage. A sign of true love is the willingness to keep to this order and wait. In such a way you honour God, your future spouse and yourself.

For some, as well, it is the seriousness of the imminent commitment that allows them to test whether it is really the right thing to get married. The run up to marriage is not only a much-needed time of preparation but can also be a time of

testing which should not be complicated by sexual activity. If you establish a mutually satisfying sexual relationship, you can lose objectivity and be fooled into marrying someone who is not right for you.

'We don't need to go through a marriage ceremony—it is only a piece of paper'
The marriage ceremony is not simply a man-made formality. God created marriage, bringing the husband and wife together in marriage (*'Therefore what God has joined together, let man not separate'*—Matthew 19:6). The vows are said to each other, before those gathered, and, most importantly, before God. God also uses marriage as a living illustration of the relationship of Christ (the Bridegroom) with his Church (the Bride) (see Ephesians 5:22-33).

The public nature of marriage makes it completely different from living together (cohabitation) (See the panel on page 28) and one does not necessarily lead to the other. Throughout the Bible marriages are publicly acknowledged and marriage still has an important public as well as personal dimension.

Marriage changes and benefits society when the couple leave their old family unit and form a new and permanent one. Such units are the building blocks of society that provide it with stability. In contrast, a large number of chaotic and ever-changing relationships will give rise to a less stable society. You may sense that society is falling apart all around; this is because marriage is being rejected by many and weakened by the rising divorce rate.

The public nature of marriage also allows both husband and wife to be held accountable for the promises they have made, makes others realize that the married couple are no longer available, and reminds the community of their responsibility to support the marriage. Marriage is also a legal contract made before witnesses.

'We need to try out the physical side before we make the big commitment of marriage'

Many people fear that not having a physical relationship before marriage will make them clumsy and inexperienced on their wedding night. However, it is actually the closeness of discovering something new together that brings much of the joy to early married sexual experience. Here is what a recently married couple said about this:

> Since being married it has become clear to us how important it is that sex should only take place within marriage. Because we waited until marriage, there is no pressure to 'perform' as neither of us have any past sexual experiences. This gives us much greater freedom to enjoy each other without the baggage of past memories.

Some are tempted to carry out a sexual 'test drive' before marriage to make sure that everything is working and compatible. In fact, sex outside marriage is so starkly different from sex inside marriage that you wouldn't be testing what you are trying to test anyway! You simply cannot try out total commitment. And God clearly warns us that this test drive may have painful consequences.

Temptation to sexual intimacy in an established and mature friendship is one reason that the Bible gives for getting married (1 Corinthians 7:36). Marriage is a protection (although not a complete one) from sexual temptation. However, such struggles can occur when marriage seems impossible. (If you are so committed to each other, consider whether marriage is really impossible or just inconvenient.) The Bible makes it quite clear that, as one writer put it, 'if you are not ready for marriage *to* one another, then you are not ready for sex *with* one another'.[7] If you have decided that marriage is not a possibility, you both need to step back from the relationship, either in intensity or completely depending how radical you have to be to avoid yourself falling. This problem is another reason why it is important to include the potential for marriage as a criterion for going out.

> **However, outside marriage we should certainly not seek out, nor give ourselves the freedom to enjoy sexual arousal.**

In summary, your response to each of the above reasons for premarital sex depends on trusting God. Learn to recognize and reject human, worldly arguments (1 Corinthians 2:13-14) even if they sometimes seem plausible. Rather be confident that the God who made you knows what is best for you. *'Trust in the LORD with all your heart and lean not on your own understanding. In all your ways acknowledge him, and he will make your paths straight'* (Proverbs 3:5,6).

THREE—If sex is for marriage, how physical should we get when we go out?

Sexual interest in the opposite sex is normal, not wrong—that is the way that God made us. Neither is sexual arousal wrong in itself—it sometimes just happens without us seeking or anticipating it. However, outside marriage we should certainly not seek out, nor give ourselves the freedom to enjoy sexual arousal.

What the Bible says about sexual purity

Sexual purity begins in the desires of our heart. Jesus said, *'But I tell you that*

Does God really know best— His plan or ours?

Studies on marriage versus living together (cohabitation)

▶ In the UK, Western Europe and United States of America, cohabitation rates have risen steadily over the last 30 years. However many studies highlight the benefits of marriage compared to living together.

▶ 'Living together' before marriage doesn't strengthen marriage. More than 70% of couples under 35 entering marriage have cohabited first. However, studies show that such marriages are more likely to end in divorce and are less likely to be happy than those where cohabitation hasn't preceded marriage. Couples who wait for marriage to have sex also enjoy sex within marriage more. Cohabitation isn't an effective way of finding out whether marriage will work.

▶ Most cohabiting relationships don't last long. The average duration of such a childless relationship in the UK is 19 months before it leads to a birth, a marriage or terminates. Still 60% marriages last for life.

▶ The instability of most cohabiting relationships has lead to many single parent families. Children born to a cohabiting couple have a 52% chance of seeing their parents split up by the age of 5 years compared to 8% who are born to married parents.

▶ Cohabitees are more likely to have an abortion, be unfaithful to their partner, get depressed, have alcohol problems and suffer domestic violence than married people.

See endnotes: 4, 5, 6

anyone who looks on a woman lustfully has already committed adultery with her in his heart' (Matthew 5:28). Jesus is warning us against feeding our inner sexual appetite through thoughts as a substitute for the act of sex. (How difficult it is to avoid these thoughts in a society where so many sexually provocative images are used as advertising in our streets.) If what Jesus says applies to our thoughts, it must also apply to our actions.

Paul exhorts the Corinthian Christians to *'flee from sexual immorality'* (1 Corinthians 6:18). In seeking sexual arousal, we will be going in exactly the opposite direction! God's Word is saying, 'Keep away from the cliff!' and we are selfishly going as close to the edge as possible because of the foolish desire to see and enjoy the view. Such an approach may reflect a wrong attitude of heart in seeing how much we can get away with.

Just the way we are made

Once we are on the road of sexual arousal, we find it is actually a steep and slippery downhill path! Once sexually aroused, our desire is for more intimacy leading to further arousal and so on. This spiral of activity and desire is meant for a purpose! It is designed to prepare the body for full sexual intercourse in the right context of marriage. If you are going out and find yourself on this path, you may have found a regular way off the path, but not without putting yourself and your girl/boyfriend under considerable strain. One day you may not find a way of stopping the slide into full intercourse with its lasting consequences and profound regrets.

What tempts one person on to the path will be different for another person and may be different for you and your girl/boyfriend. For some, kissing is too provocative. For others, even simply holding hands may encourage unhelpful or sinful thoughts. You need to ask yourself regularly whether what you are thinking, doing, provoking or seeking is consistent with an inner desire for a pure life that honours God. Jesus tells us that in order to escape sin's misery and judgement, it is worth rooting out anything that causes us to sin (Matthew 5:29).

> **Once we are on the road of sexual arousal, we find it is actually a steep and slippery downhill path! Once sexually aroused, our desire is for more intimacy leading to further arousal and so on.**

Consider as well the context in which you may be tempted. Perhaps these are times when you are less accountable such as being alone in the house together, or when keeping your self-control is less

easy due to alcohol or tiredness. It may be good to discuss between yourselves what is helpful to avoid (better in an unheated moment or it may make temptation worse). Guys should remember that a girl's desire for emotional security may lead her to agree to a level of physical intimacy that is not right before marriage. Girls should remember that you can lead your boyfriend into sin by being unthinkingly provocative in your appearance and behaviour.

What happens if you don't keep sexual activity for marriage...?

There can be a high price to pay for straying away from God's plan for sexual activity. Your emotions, your body, your relationship, and the closeness of your walk with God may all come under threat.

You will hurt

The expression 'one flesh' is very descriptive—it means that through sex we can and should become so close to our husband or wife (emotionally, physically and spiritually) that nothing on earth can separate us. Sex is a strong bond like glue that binds the husband and wife together and strengthens the relationship. This is a bond that was not designed to be broken. When it is broken, it always hurts and damages those involved. This can give rise to a wide range of painful emotions in ourselves and towards others—for example regret, guilt, anger, sadness, depression and loss of self-confidence. Here is the testimony of Jane who looks back at her first relationship:

'As a fourteen-year-old girl going out with an older boy, I felt having sex was what was expected. It was not a great relationship and ended in two months. I am now twenty-eight and still feel the pain and regret of having given away something so special to someone who was not in a position to treasure it. Looking back, he has shared something of me that I should never have chosen to give him.'

Because it is *ourselves* that is given away in sexual union, it is our very heart, our value and identity, which is threatened so much if sex is abused. Sex involves utter vulnerability to another person. Without the security of absolute commitment we are wide open to painful rejection and loss of trust. This can have dramatic effects on our state of mind and confidence as well as future relationships, as Ivan experienced:

> I first had intercourse with my girlfriend when we were fifteen. I'd been going out with her for almost a year, and loved her very much. She was friendly, outgoing, charismatic. We'd done everything but have intercourse, and then one night she asked if we could go all the way.

> A few days later, we broke up. It was the most painful time in my life. I had opened myself up to her more than I had to anybody, even my parents. I was depressed, moody, nervous. My friends dropped me because I was so unsociable. I felt a failure. I dropped out of sports. I started to fail at school.

> I didn't go out with anyone for ages. I was afraid of falling in love.

Sex involves utter vulnerability to another person. Without the security of absolute commitment we are wide open to painful rejection and loss of trust.

The outcome of Ivan's relationship is not uncommon. Teenage relationships outside marriage frequently break up soon after sex has taken place. Often, unlike the situation for Ivan, it is the guy who walks away. There can be various reasons for this. He may have had his thrill and now wants to move on to the next challenge, or he may take fright at the greater level of commitment that the girl often demands once she has given herself fully to him physically.

Complete physical surrender without the complete and loving life-long commitment of marriage is inconsistent and sooner or later will break you up spiritually and emotionally. We, as paediatricians, see the effects of this in the young people we care for in our clinics and schools. Such damage can produce a

range of physical symptoms such as headaches and tummy aches as well as effects of low self-esteem such as self-harm and eating disorders. If people experience the pain of the sexual bond repeatedly forming and breaking, they may try to protect themselves from the pain by (often subconsciously) trying to toughen themselves up emotionally. Like the scars of a wound, we will hurt or we will harden. But there is hope. There is one route to genuine healing of these scars—through the forgiveness and love of the Lord Jesus. Only he can heal our pain and soften our hardness.

And sometimes the Lord graciously uses our sins in this area to draw us to himself. Here is Tom's testimony:

As a Christian, I remain saddened by and ashamed of my past sexual experiences. But it was these that led me to long for a pure life and eventually brought me to my knees to ask for and receive forgiveness from the Lord Jesus. It is amazing to think that he was willing to use the depths of my sin to save me! Perhaps no other sin would have shaken me to repent.

You may get (her) pregnant

The oneness of sex is fully expressed when the sperm and egg unite to form new life. In the era of contraception, it is easy to forget that God designed sex to produce babies, and marriages to be fruitful. None of the commonly used contraceptives can guarantee to prevent this happening! Fourteen per cent of couples who 'typically'[8] use the condom conceive unintentionally in the first year of their relationship.[9] Unplanned encounters have much higher rates of pregnancy. And you don't have to have full sexual intercourse to get pregnant.

There is hope. There is one route to genuine healing of these scars—through the forgiveness and love of the Lord Jesus.

It may be stating the obvious that bringing up a child is a demanding and a long-term responsibility. It is God's design that a baby grows up in the security of a family. Both parents have a God-given responsibility for bringing up their children. This is another important reason for keeping sex for marriage.

You may get a sexually transmitted infection[10]

Another consequence of sex outside marriage is catching a sexually transmitted infection (STI). The rising number of sexual partners has lead to a rapid spread of these infections around the world, especially amongst young people. Rates of infection for the most common STI, Chlamydia, are rising fast with a three-fold increase in the last eight years[11].

Remember that the only way of being sure of a marriage without STIs is for the husband and wife to come to it without any previous sexual intimacy and to remain faithful within marriage.

The spread of STIs has not been contained by easier access to condoms and more teaching about their use. The increasing availability has actually increased spread of STIs by encouraging sexual activity outside marriage because people think (wrongly) that they can have 'safe(r) sex'.[12] (See panel on page 37.)

34

You may threaten your spiritual life

Though the physical consequences of 'going too far' may be huge and long-lasting, there is something even more serious at stake than this. Jesus tells us that our spiritual health is more important than our physical health because it has an eternal significance. *'Do not be afraid of those who kill the body but cannot kill the soul. Rather, be afraid of the one who can destroy both soul and body in hell'* (Matthew 10:28).

Physical intimacy before marriage takes away a God-given innocence and makes us feel guilty—this is our conscience warning us that we are over-stepping God's boundaries. Such an awareness is clear from Mary's testimony when she was encouraged by her boyfriend to go too far:

> *When you had been physically intimate with your boyfriend, how did you feel afterwards?*

Mainly I felt guilty and ashamed, particularly with my first boyfriend. It was the first time I had crossed those boundaries and my conscience was not yet hardened. I kept thinking other people (especially my parents) would know simply by looking at me, because I felt so different. I was also worried that my boyfriend would think differently of me and that he would lose interest in me as a person.

Sexually Transmitted Infections (STIs)-Did you know?

▶ Most people with an STI do not know it.

▶ The most common STI in the UK and USA is Chlamydia. This infection is often unnoticed but by blocking up the woman's genital tract, the first signs may only become apparent several years later with infertility problems.

▶ Women are more susceptible to STIs than men because they have a larger surface area susceptible to infection. Adolescent females are at highest risk. Women also suffer more health complications of STIs than men.

▶ All STIs can be transmitted by oral sex.

▶ Those with one STI are more susceptible to another especially HIV. Each year, about 1,000 women die in the UK and 4,000 women die in the USA from cervical cancer. Probably all of these cancers were caused by earlier wart virus infection caught through sexual contact.

▶ Several STIs, including herpes and wart virus are not curable with medicines and may be life-long.

Do you think it affected your spiritual life at all?

I mentioned that I felt different. The truth is that I was different. I had disobeyed God just as Adam and Eve had done in the Garden of Eden. Like them I had lost my innocence because I had experienced things he had never intended me to experience at that time in my life.

Persisting in disobedience paralyses our spiritual growth and our ability to be effective for God. We are threatening the very home of the Holy Spirit when we sin sexually. *'… he who sins sexually sins against his own body. Do you not know that your body is a temple of the Holy Spirit, who is in you, whom you have received from God?'* (1 Corinthians 6:18-19).

Here is how Mary described it:
My church and youth group attendance suffered. Part of this was due to the 'exclusiveness' of the relationship. I would say it is always a bad sign if you want

to spend more and more time alone together. Relationships should always be open to the light of God's Word and to the observance of godly people. I began to read my Bible less and pray less, and most of my prayers became self-centred. I seemed to spend all my time repenting and yet would find myself doing the same things I had repented of very soon after.

You may damage your relationship

Opposite to what many people think, exerting physical self-control helps rather than hinders a relationship. We have already seen that the emphasis in going out should not be on physical intimacy—if you are constantly wanting to go as far as you can in physical involvement, your motives and practices in the relationship are wrong. It is hard, if not impossible, to get to know someone and decide if your characters, interests and futures are compatible when you are preoccupied with physical intimacy.

Self-control allows you to enjoy the relationship free from physical distractions and a sense of guilt and will enable you to test the relationship out effectively. It will allow you to grow individually and together without compromise from the *sin that so easily entangles'* (Hebrews 12:1).

Condoms and the myth of safe(r) sex

▶ Condoms reduce the risk of infection-they don't protect from any STI 100% of the time.

▶ There is no evidence of reduced spread of the warts virus even with 100% condom use. There is some evidence of protection from some consequences of infection including genital warts in men and cervical cancer in women. Condoms prevent spread poorly because the virus is often found outside the area covered by the condom.

▶ There is no evidence of reduction in sexual transmission of the STI Trichomonas with 100% condom use.

▶ Gonorrhoea and Chlamydia transmission are only reduced by about 50% with 100% condom use.

▶ About 25% of adolescents report alcohol or drug use during their most recent sexual experience, which compromised their ability to use a condom correctly.

Thinking of the future?

Look ahead and make a determined decision to keep sex and all that leads up to full intercourse for marriage. Hear again from Jane who is now in her twenties and looks back wishing that she had thought ahead about this important issue before the pressure of a relationship persuaded her to do something wrong:

> I had a sexual relationship with a boyfriend when I was fourteen years old, at a time when I had not thought much about my own ideas on sex—whether it was right or wrong and what I really wanted in my life. I now see the huge impact that decision has had on my life. I see how important it is to make decisions about these things before getting into a relationship where the pressure to say 'yes' can be massive.

The self-discipline that you learn will have lasting benefits. If you end up marrying, the holding back now will enrich your marriage because your partner will sense the security that comes from your self-control. Guys are especially likely to be tempted to push the boundaries so that their girlfriend is always having to say 'no'. If this is the case and they get married, she may find it difficult to change her 'role' and relax in a truly fulfilling sexual relationship. And by acting in a pure way now, you will *'keep your marriage bed pure'* (see Hebrews 13:4), whether or not you decide to marry your current girl/boyfriend.

Finally, let us hear from Michael, who looks back over more than thirty years of married life:

> The companionship, which my wife and I have shared, has become deeper with time. By sharing the times of great happiness, such as our wedding and later the birth of our children, as well as facing difficulties together, our relationship of love and trust has grown stronger.
>
> Security in our marriage has been a product of being faithful, being thoughtful and being forgiving. It has been good to resolve any tensions, before going to

sleep, by apologizing and asking forgiveness for wrongs done. The strength of our mutual love has produced a secure home for our children. The security of our family home has been shared with others as we have reached out to our neighbours, our children and our children's friends.

> **The Bible makes it clear that singleness is a gift which all Christians have until they receive the other gift of marriage.**

Imperfect as we are, we have known Christ's daily forgiveness in our lives and our marriage. The intimate bond of a sexual relationship was worth the waiting for. The sacredness of this unique relationship has been part of the cement that has held our marriage together.

If we keep our best for marriage and give our best to marriage, then marriage will not disappoint us.

Singleness—A realistic alternative to marriage[13]

The Bible makes it clear that singleness is a gift which all Christians have until they receive the other gift of marriage (1 Corinthians 7:7). Being single allows the Christian to serve the Lord in a way that is impossible for the married person. Paul writes, *'I would like you to be free from concern. An unmarried man is concerned about the Lord's affairs—how he can please the Lord. But a married man is concerned about the affairs of this world—how he can please his wife— and his interests are divided'* (1 Corinthians 7: 32-34). Read on in this passage for similar advice to the unmarried woman. For the committed Christian, the single state with all its freedom is not a gift to be given up lightly and some people are called by God to be single for life (Matthew 19:12).

Sometimes those around a single person are reluctant to see the benefits of such singleness. These may be more obvious to the person him/herself. Remember that the whole church is blessed when someone, through singleness, lives a life of undivided service to the Lord. Mark writes:

> I have often experienced the well-intentioned pressure of family and friends, who assume, often without saying so, that singleness is abnormal and should be avoided at all costs. Yet, as someone who has lead a chaste life, I know that I would not have been able to achieve the many things for God that I have, if I had been married with a family. The demands of work and family would have been irreconcilable.

> I have experienced times of loneliness (though I know of some ill-matched and unsatisfactory marriages that are desperately lonely). However, I have learnt the importance of trusted and godly friends and with this provision my single life has been very fulfilling. No life outside God's will can fulfil. The important thing is to find contentment in the situation in life to which God has called us.

Other issues

Pornography

The internet has made it easy to look at pornography without anyone else knowing. Nowadays many films and popular magazines also contain provocative visual material. Christians are not immune from temptations from these sources. Here are several reasons why using pornography is wrong and highly damaging:

▶ Jesus warns us that lusting after someone in our minds and hearts is sinful (Matthew 5:28). As with other sins, it deadens our walk with the Lord and dries up the fruitfulness of our lives.

▶ By its nature pornography crudely snips up a person, separating the object of our lust (not just in the image but in our minds) from the reality of the person—their lives, thoughts, needs, situation and how we relate to them. Once our mind becomes used to this, it can affect all kinds of relationships that we have.

▶ This is all done for our selfish entertainment. The use of pornography is highly self-absorbing and self-centred.

▶ Pornography can be addictive. There is a hunger for more and more provocative images to produce the same stimulation. When indecency on the paper or in film fails to provoke, the person who uses pornography may turn to people with the frightening desire to de-humanise them for his own selfish ends. This process has lead to many horrific crimes in recent years including the actions of several serial murderers.

> **...beware of pornography. If you are tempted in this area, take radical action.**
> (MATTHEW 5:29-30)

So beware of pornography. If you are tempted in this area, take radical action (Matthew 5:29-30). Make yourself accountable to a church leader or trustworthy friend who can, if necessary, challenge you in this area as well as provide encouragement and prayer support. Change the environment of your home so that others are always around when you are on the internet (be careful of computers in unsupervised bedrooms). Make sure there is a high-level filter on all your internet access. Most importantly ask God to forgive you of past sins in this area and then resolve in his strength to be obedient.

Masturbation

The Bible does not directly refer to masturbation. However, we commented earlier that you should avoid seeking sexual arousal with someone you are going out with. The reasons for guarding against this also helpfully apply to self-arousal. Consider the following, too:

▶ Masturbation separates a sexual act from a relationship, whereas God plans sexual activity to take place only within marriage.
▶ We should not ignore our conscience's witness. Many testify to a sense of unease and guilt about masturbating.
▶ Although often used to relieve sexual tension, it can arouse sexual interest and fantasies, which tempt one to increasing sexual activity outside marriage.

Most people don't talk about masturbation because it is embarrassing, so you may not realize that many Christians struggle with temptation in this area. If this is a problem for you, God promises his strength and help. *'I can do everything through him who gives me strength'* (Philippians 4:13).

Homosexuality

Some young people have a sexual interest in those of the same sex. This is usually a passing interest as the person grows and matures. However, for some (a small minority) such an interest remains. The Bible makes it quite clear that giving in to such sexual interest by pursuing homosexual thoughts and actions is wrong, and has serious physical and spiritual consequences (Romans 1:26-27). Biologically and physically, it goes against the way God created people to be.

If you are troubled by homosexual thoughts, it is sometimes easier to accept the world's view that homosexuality is natural, and that there is nothing wrong with it, but this is clearly against God's teaching in the Bible. Rather than taking what may seem the easier way out, turn to a church leader or trustworthy friend who can provide prayer support, encouragement and accountability. You could also contact a Christian organization such as the True Freedom Trust (www.tftrust.u-net.com) which encourages people, with God's help, to overcome homosexual temptation.

If we confess our sins, he is faithful and just and will forgive us our sins and purify us from all unrighteousness

1 John 1:9

What to do if you have made mistakes

Here is the final part of Mary's testimony:

> I became convinced that God couldn't possibly still love me because I was such an awful person. It took years for me to believe that God could forgive me when I had truly repented. It also took years for me to realize that, in the midst of my sin, he loved me still. That still amazes me.

Reading this booklet may have left you with an unpleasant awareness of guilt before God. If so, you join a very large number of other Christian brothers and sisters—indeed none of us is sexually innocent. You may even think that your sins have been too serious or too persistent for you to receive forgiveness from God. It is tempting to respond to this sense of guilt by crawling away in despair or trying to ignore it in the hope that it will disappear.

Those who have fallen short of God's standard through sexual sin can know complete forgiveness because Jesus has already paid the full price for our sin when he died on the cross.

The Christian good news is the only and complete answer to this awareness of guilt, however serious your sins. It offers the hope of forgiveness and a new start. Those who have fallen short of God's standard through sexual sin can know complete forgiveness because Jesus has already paid the full price for our sin when he died on the cross.

Remember, too, Paul's words of great assurance to the Roman Christians: *'Therefore, there is now no condemnation for those who are in Christ Jesus, because through Christ Jesus the law of the Spirit of life set me free from the law of sin and death'* (Romans 8:1-2). If you have been saved by the Lord Jesus, then you will not face condemnation on Judgement Day for what you have done.

Jesus is the only answer to the mistakes that we have all made. And when you recognize that you have not lived up to God's standards, he requires that you do something definite in response:

▶ You need to say 'sorry' to God for what you have done, and ask him to forgive you through Jesus' death on the cross.

▶ You need to resolve before God not to make the same mistakes again. That is what repentance means—a true turning round to God asking him to motivate you to be obedient in your actions and strengthen you to resist all future temptation.

▶ Remember that this resolution will mean taking practical steps to avoid all similar temptations in the future (e.g. deciding on boundaries in a relationship, getting rid of a computer that is the source of temptation).

▶ You should say sorry to those you have hurt, if this is possible.

▶ You should look for a fellow Christian to whom you can be accountable in this area.

'If we confess our sins, he is faithful and just and will forgive us our sins and purify us from all unrighteousness' (1 John 1:9).

Dr Chris Richards and Dr Liz Jones

For a more in-depth look at the subject, we recommend 'The Relationships Revolution' by Nigel Pollock, published by IVP (1998).

SEEKING PURITY

TEN REASONS
to keep sex for marriage
and avoid deliberate sexual arousal outside marriage

1. God made you—he knows how you work. If your designer and creator says that marriage is the only right place for sexual activity, it is worth paying attention.

2. God says, 'Flee from sexual immorality' (1 Corinthians 6:18). The word translated 'immorality' means all forms of sexual intimacy outside marriage.

3. A life of obedience will honour God (1 Corinthians 6:20).

4. You are threatening the home of the Holy Spirit when you sin sexually (1 Corinthians 6:18-19).

5. A life of obedience will bring lasting fruitfulness for his kingdom (John 15:1-11).

6. It is hard, if not impossible, to get to know someone and decide if your characters, interests and futures are compatible when you are preoccupied with physical intimacy.

7. Avoid the life-long shame and pain of extra-marital sexual experience that many have suffered.

8. Avoid risking sexually transmitted infections. Avoid the shame and fear of bringing these infections into your marriage.

9. Avoid getting pregnant at the wrong time.

10. Think of the future. Do you want to enter marriage with a 'past'? Or do you want to enter marriage with the innocent joy of discovering for the first time the rich secrets of sexual intimacy?

It can be difficult to say 'No'; but think about what happens if you say 'Yes'.

TWO STATES OF LIFE THAT ARE PLEASING TO GOD

(Matthew 19:3-12)

EITHER—Singleness

A gift from God	1 Corinthians 7:7
Necessarily sexually inactive = 'Eunuch'	Matthew 19:12
Some need to be	Matthew 19:12a
Some choose to be for the kingdom	Matthew 19:12b
More readily allowing whole-hearted work	
for the Lord than marriage	1 Corinthians 7:32-35

OR—Marriage

Created by God		Genesis 2:24 and
		Matthew 19:4-5
A gift from God		1 Corinthians 7:7
Purposes	To provide companionship	Genesis 2:18
	To produce children	Genesis 4:1
	To illustrate God's love for his church	Ephesians 5:25-32
Another benefit	Protection from sexual temptation	1 Corinthians 7:36
Lifelong		Matthew 19:6b
Between man and woman		Matthew 19:4-5
Only one husband or wife		1 Corinthians 7:2
To be honoured by all		Hebrews 13:4,
		Proverbs 5:18-20
Christian should marry Christian		2 Corinthians 6:14
Demanding on time and energy		1 Corinthians 7:32-35
For this world only (i.e. not in heaven)		Matthew 22:30

SEX IS

Created by God		Genesis 2:24
A good gift from God		Genesis 1:31
Only for marriage		Genesis 2:24,
		Ephesians 5:3
		and Hebrews 13:4
Purposes	To strengthen marriage	Genesis 2:24
	To produce children	Genesis 4:1

BAD CONSEQUENCES OF SEX OUTSIDE MARRIAGE

Blessings of obedience compared to curses of disobedience	Deuteronomy 30:15-20
David's adultery with Bathsheba has spiritual, family and political consequences	2 Samuel 12:1-15
Spiritual—becoming ineffective for the Lord	1 Corinthians 6:18-19 and Mark 4:18-19
Spiritual—the bondage of sexual sin	Proverbs 5:20-23
Spiritual and physical death	Proverbs 6:32 and 7:21-27
Social downfall	Proverbs 5:7-14

GODLY ATTITUDES IN RELATIONSHIPS

Seek God and his commands above everything	Matthew 6:33
Seek sexual purity	Psalm 119:9, Ephesians 5:3, 1 Corinthians 6:18
Seek God's strength to be obedient	Philippians 4:13
Trust God's wisdom, not your own	Proverbs 3:5-8
Trust God's good provision for his own	Psalm 23
Be prayerful	Matthew 6:5-15
Be loving and forgiving	Colossians 3:12-14 1 Corinthians 13
Be content in your situation	Philippians 4:10-13
Take advice from the spiritually wise around you	Proverbs 12:15 and 22:17
Avoid rash commitments	Proverbs 20:25

ENDNOTES

1 See 'Marriage Works', J.John, Authentic Publications, 2002, for a fuller coverage of this issue

2 Quoted from 'The Relationships Revolution', Nigel Pollock, IVP, 1998, p 96.

3 See 'Marriage—Sex in the Service of God', Christopher Ash, IVP, 2003, pp 214-216 for a detailed study on the meaning of this word.

4 'Marriage-lite The Rise of Cohabitation and its Consequences', Patricia Morgan, ISCS 2000.

5 'Does Marriage Matter?' Civitas, 2004

6 See also http://members.aol.com/cohabiting for an extensive summary of studies looking at the differences between cohabitation and marriage.

7 Quoted from 'God, Sex and Marriage', John Richardson, St Matthias Press, 1998. An excellent and readable study of 1 Corinthians 7

8 'Typical use' estimates include inconsistent use, incorrect use, breakage and slippage

9 Workshop Summary: Scientific Evidence on Condom Effectiveness for STD Prevention. July 20 2001. Available at http://www.niaid.nih.gov/dmid/stds/condomreport.pdf

10 See 'Sex, Condoms and STDs: What We Need to Know' available from The Medical Institute on http://www.medinstitute.org

11 See the UK Government's Health Protection Agency website at http://www.hpa.org.uk under 'Sexually Transmitted Infections'

12 Workshop Summary: Scientific Evidence on Condom Effectiveness for STD Prevention. July 20 2001. Available at http://www.niaid.nih.gov/dmid/stds/condomreport.pdf

13 See 'The Single Issue', Al Hsu, IVP, 1998, for a fuller coverage of this issue

QUESTIONS AND ANSWERS ABOUT LOVEWISE

The two authors of this booklet, Dr Chris Richards and Dr Liz Jones, are presenters and trustees for a charity called Lovewise. Here they explain what Lovewise is about:

What is Lovewise?

Lovewise was set up in 2002. It sends presenters into schools and youth groups to teach about marriage, sex and relationships from a Christian perspective. The  presentations use Powerpoint slides, video interviews and personal testimonies. Most presentations have so far been in the north east of England but we are in the process of setting up further UK teams so that many more may receive them. Our presentation material is also available to individual class teachers and youth group leaders around the country who are sympathetic to the aims of Lovewise and are able to sign our Statement of Faith and Code of Practice. There is a range of presentations for different school years and some with greater biblical content have been prepared especially for church youth groups.

Why was Lovewise formed?

Many young people in our society have not had the opportunity to hear that there is an alternative to the 'safer sex' message, which is being so actively promoted by the government and many health agencies. So we formed Lovewise, which helps young people to consider the alternative—to positively aspire to the life-long commitment of marriage and to wait for sex until marriage. We believe that our Creator's instructions can help young people to know how to live wisely.

What issues do your presentations cover and who gives them?

A typical schools presentation addresses the following topics:

▶ the pressure that comes from the media and peers;

▶ the goodness and benefits of marriage;

▶ marriage as the only right place for sexual intimacy;

▶ why sex outside marriage can never be completely 'safe';

▶ advice on how to avoid sexual intimacy when going out.

Our presentation team in the north east consists of fourteen presenters, and

 we usually give presentations in pairs. Some, but not all the team, have a medical background—our team includes one journalist and several teachers as well as a mother of four. Recently several students have joined us, including Anika, photographed here with her husband Matt.

How can your school or youth group receive Lovewise presentations?

Our teams of presenters are limited in number and coverage at the moment. However, we would like to hear from you, or your parents, youth group leader or teacher if you would be interested in receiving some of our presentations. It may be that one of your teachers or youth leaders would be able to give the presentation or we may be able to form a team in your area. You can contact us by e-mailing us on info@lovewise.org.uk or writing to Lovewise, 25 Brandling Place South, Jesmond, Newcastle upon Tyne NE2 4RU.

NOTES

NOTES

NOTES

NOTES

University: the real challenge

WISE
CHOICES

ANDREW KING
64 PAGES
£3
1 903087 82 1

Is university a good thing for young Christians? Is it a great maturing process, a time of spiritual growth and evangelism? Or is it a time of overwhelming worldly influence, compromise and drifting away from God? Well, it should and can be the former: a good time to grow spiritually and serve God well. But there are very real dangers to be avoided. This booklet will help prospective students, parents and churches to prepare to cope with and, where possible, to avoid some key dangers, as well as to make the very most of the wonderful opportunities student life affords!

REFERENCE UC

University: The real Challenge is not merely a survival guide for the potential overwhelmings of university life, but a timely and deeply biblical resource to help prospective students flourish in the academy, yet without being marginalized. As it turns out, university need not be a detriment to the Christian student's faith and devotion. In Andrew King's view, a little Scripture-grounded guidance and a regular dose of the Gospel transforms even the most hostile university campus into a sanctifying setting for believers.
John J. Bombaro, Ph.D. Director, The John Newton International Center for Christian Studies and Fellow, Dickinson College, Carlisle, Pennsylvania, USA

Christian students leaving home for university invariably find this experience their first and most challenging rite of passage.

Andrew King's insights into university life from his own experience serve to make this book an indispensable tool to students and those who work with them.

Geoff Thomas, Pastor, Alfred Place Baptist Church, Aberystwyth, Wales

This short and easy-to-read book is filled with biblical common sense. Every Christian young person going to university will find it worth reading.

Stuart Olyott, Pastoral Director of the Evangelical Movement of Wales

Thoroughly biblical, short, easy-to-read and very well applied—I am delighted to commend this booklet! If only two of my school friends had read it before they went to university and shipwrecked their Christian lives. I really am going to give a copy of this to each of my godchildren.

Rico Tice, Associate Minister (Evangelism), All Souls Church, Langham Place, London

This booklet will help students greatly because it describes key biblical principles in a succinct manner.

Dr Stuart Burgess, Head of the Department of Mechanical Engineering, Bristol University

AVAILABLE FROM CHRISTIAN BOOKSHOPS,
OR BY CALLING DAY ONE: 01568 613 740.

sales@dayone.co.uk   dayone.co.uk

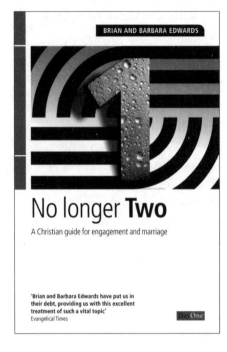

No Longer Two
A Christian guide for engagement and marriage

BRIAN AND BARBARA EDWARDS
LARGE FORMAT PAPERBACK
144 PAGES
£7
1 903087 00 7

With more than one in three marriages ending in divorce, the institution is more under threat than ever and divorce among Christians is at an all time high. In response to this, churches now offer pre-marital counselling for engaged couples. Some clergy now refuse to marry a couple unless they have taken such a course. 'No Longer Two' is a highly acclaimed marriage preparation guide offering an exciting way of working together to build a strong marriage based upon the clear teaching and common sense of the Bible. Whether or not you are familiar with the Bible, you will find this an easy-to-use guide—perfect for individuals and groups alike.

REFERENCE: NL2

Quite simply one of the best books on the market today on the subject of marriage
THE MONTHLY RECORD

'Brian and Barbara Edwards have put us in their debt, providing us with this excellent treatment of such a vital topic'
EVANGELICAL TIMES

What's so special about No Longer Two?

Thorough treatment: chapter by chapter the subject is dealt with from the Bible with practical application

Bible studies ensure that the reader actually has to get involved—perfect for individuals, great for groups.

AVAILABLE FROM CHRISTIAN BOOKSHOPS,
OR BY CALLING DAY ONE: 01568 613 740.

sales@dayone.co.uk   dayone.co.uk

This book is published in conjunction with **Lovewise**.
Lovewise is a registered charity that provides presentations in schools and youth groups on the subject of marriage, sex and relationships from a Christian perspective. It has also developed material for use by teachers and youth group leaders. Turn to pages 54 and 55 for more information on Lovewise.

Lovewise
25 Brandling Place South
Jesmond
Newcastle upon Tyne
NE2 4RU
email: info@lovewise.org.uk

© Dr Chris Richards and Dr Liz Jones 2005
All Bible references are from the NIV unless otherwise stated.
Fictitious names have been used for all quotes which have been provided confidentially.

First printed 2005

All Scripture quotations are taken from the New International Version.

A CIP record is held at The British Library   ISBN 1 903087 87 2

Published by Day One Publications Ryelands Road, Leominster, HR6 8NZ

☎ 01568 613 740 **FAX** 01568 611 473   email: sales@dayone.co.uk
www.dayone.co.uk

Editor: Jim Holmes

Design and Art Direction: Steve Devane Illustrations: Susan LeVan
Printed by Gutenberg Press, Malta